by Tamara Cufrin
illustrated by Laure Fournier

SCHOOL PUBLISHERS

Printed in China

ISBN 10: 0-15-351522-8
ISBN 13: 978-0-15-351522-4

Ordering Options
ISBN 10: 0-15-351214-8 (Grade 4 Advanced Collection)
ISBN 13: 978-0-15-351214-8 (Grade 4 Advanced Collection)
ISBN 10: 0-15-358112-5 (package of 5)
ISBN 13: 978-0-15-358112-0 (package of 5)

3 4 5 6 7 8 9 10 985 12 11 10 09 08

At the basketball court in the park, Benito Juarez dribbled the ball and stared calmly into the eyes of his opponents. "Who's going to stop me?" Benito asked confidently. He scanned the defenders, looking to see which ones he could pass between.

Just then four players surged forward, forming a wall. "Ha!" Benito said and then responded swiftly. He sped to his right, taking his defenders with him, and then cut back to the left. He was far too quick for any of them, and he easily moved to the hoop and laid the ball into it. "Two more points for Benito!" he yelled.

The other players looked down, defeated once again. "Hey guys, how about improving your skills so that I can have some decent competition?" Benito laughed.

"I've had enough, Benito. I'm going home," replied Raul, who lived in the neighborhood.

"Oh, tired of losing to Benito, Raul?" Benito asked with a smile. Raul didn't smile back. He realized that Benito was an excellent basketball player. Like others who played with him, Raul was getting tired of Benito's constant bragging. "Hey, Raul, how about I let Jaime play on your team so it's all of you against me? Then will you play some more?"

"Sure, Benito, because that gives me a better chance of beating you," replied Raul.

They started a new game, this time five against one, but it didn't take Benito long to defeat the other team. As the others walked off the court, Benito snickered, "No one beats Benito!" His words resounded throughout the park.

Benito headed home, dribbling his basketball and feeling really good about himself. It was a lovely spring day, late May, and Benito was looking forward to a long summer of winning countless basketball games on the park's courts.

As he turned down his street, he spotted his Uncle Carlos sitting on the front step with his mother. "I wonder what Uncle Carlos is doing here?" Benito thought to himself.

Uncle Carlos was a forest ranger at Redwood National Park. Benito walked toward Uncle Carlos, who turned and looked at him. "There he is," Uncle Carlos exclaimed.

"Hi, Uncle Carlos," replied Benito, and they shook hands.

"You're late for dinner again," said Benito's mother.

"Sorry, Mamma, I was winning again at the park," Benito declared proudly. Uncle Carlos held out his hands for the basketball, and Benito flipped the ball to him.

"You're good?" Uncle Carlos asked, gazing at the ball.

"I'm the best, and, in fact, I just beat five guys *all at once*," Benito boasted. Uncle Carlos tossed the ball back to Benito.

"So, you can dribble and score?" asked Uncle Carlos.

"You'll have to come and watch me play," replied Benito. He pretended to shoot the ball as Uncle Carlos watched quietly but did not smile.

"Let's go eat," said Benito's mother.

"Benito needs fuel so that he can play more great basketball!" said Benito.

As Benito's mother served the food, she glanced over at Uncle Carlos and asked, "How's everything going up there with the redwood trees?"

"Do you just ride around in a truck all day?" asked Benito.

"So, you think my job is easy?" Uncle Carlos asked Benito.

"It seems like it, I mean, I can probably do it, and I'm not even a forest ranger."

"Well, now you've got me thinking, Mr. Great Benito. I believe you have a summer vacation coming up, and maybe you'd like to spend part of it with me doing my 'easy' job," said Uncle Carlos.

Benito's mother and uncle talked about the arrangements and the trip was all set.

When the day came for Benito to go to Redwood National Park, he was not in a particularly good mood. "I was planning to spend my entire summer on the court," he said somewhat grumpily.

"You've had plenty of time on the court, and you'll have more time when you return," his mother replied. As they unzipped Benito's bag to make sure he had all of his supplies, Uncle Carlos arrived.

"Ready to go, Benito?" he asked, striding up the sidewalk to the house.

"I guess so," replied Benito as he picked up his bag and the basketball that was next to it.

"Oh, you're not going to need that," said Uncle Carlos. "There aren't any basketball courts in the middle of the woods." Benito frowned and then kissed and hugged his mother good-bye.

On the flight from Los Angeles to Redwood National Park, Benito and Uncle Carlos listened to music and had some small conversations. "You know, there's more to life than playing basketball," Uncle Carlos commented.

"Not to me," replied Benito as he stared glumly out the window.

"Well, what else do you like to do?" wondered Uncle Carlos.

"Nothing else, really, just listening to music, going to the movies, stuff like that," said Benito.

"Have you ever actually been in the woods?" asked Uncle Carlos.

"No, but I'm not scared because I can handle anything," said Benito proudly.

"We'll certainly see about that," replied Uncle Carlos. Benito didn't reply. He just gazed out the window and thought sadly about all of the basketball games he was missing at home.

9

Benito and Uncle Carlos finally arrived at the park. Uncle Carlos decided that the best way for Benito to experience the redwoods was for them to camp out for a few days. They were unloading the trunk when a swarm of mosquitoes attacked them.

Uncle Carlos smiled calmly and suggested, "Here, put on some bug cream and try to ignore them."

"There are hundreds of them!" hollered Benito, slapping the bugs off of his arms and legs.

"Hey, I thought you could handle anything," Uncle Carlos commented, but Benito didn't bother to reply. As Benito kept slapping at the bugs, Uncle Carlos built a campfire. "Sit here and let the smoke hit you, and it'll keep the bugs away." Benito did as his uncle suggested, and soon he was free of bugs.

After sitting by the fire for a few minutes, Uncle Carlos announced, "I'm going to take a little hike to get more firewood, so please set up the tent."

Benito began to work on the tent, but it was certainly no easy task. He accidentally got the ropes all twisted up and had to stop to untangle them.

When Uncle Carlos finally returned with a load of wood, he inspected the tent. "Uh, Benito, it looks like you had some problems here," he said. Benito just hung his head and said nothing because he felt really embarrassed.

Then he realized that if he pulled the ropes taut the tent would not be rumpled anymore. Finally, the tent was up and looking good!

The next morning, Uncle Carlos woke Benito up incredibly early. He told him that today they'd see the big redwood trees.

They ate a simple breakfast, packed a small bag of supplies, and began to hike through the brush. When they stopped to take a rest, Benito thought he heard something lurking in the bushes.

"What is it?" he asked anxiously.

"Why don't you go see?" asked Uncle Carlos.

"No way!" said Benito, and Uncle Carlos laughed out loud.

"*Benito can do anything*! Remember when you said that?" asked Uncle Carlos, still chuckling. Benito was reluctant to admit that he said that because, if he did, he knew that Uncle Carlos would make him go into the bushes to prove his words.

When they finally came to the base of a huge redwood tree, Benito couldn't take his eyes off of the massive tree.

"Now *that* is something great," declared Uncle Carlos. Benito thought about what his uncle said and realized that his "great" victories on the court didn't seem so great compared to this tree.

"Uncle Carlos, I agree with you completely," replied Benito. Uncle Carlos smiled, knowing that Benito was starting to understand.

"Now let me ask you a question, Benito, and please listen closely. Do you hear that redwood tree telling everyone how great she is?" Uncle Carlos inquired.

"Not at all," Benito said, without hesitating. He realized that Uncle Carlos had just taught him another important lesson: it's not good to brag.

Two weeks later, Benito Juarez returned to Los Angeles a new person. His mother noticed the change in him the moment he walked through the door. He didn't walk like a show-off. Instead he carried himself more like Uncle Carlos, and there was a new look of pride on his face.

"Benito, you look terrific!" she exclaimed, hugging him.

"Mamma, the great Benito of the basketball court no longer exists!" he declared, looking directly into her eyes.

"Well, then who is this strong young man in my house?" she asked playfully.

"It is Benito of the redwood forest. The strong Benito who no longer needs to boast or brag!" he said proudly. Benito, his mother, and Uncle Carlos all laughed out loud.

Think Critically

1. What problem did Benito have? What helped him solve the problem?

2. What words would you use to describe Benito at the beginning of this story?

3. Why was Raul tired of playing basketball with Benito?

4. Why do you think Benito's mom invited Uncle Carlos to visit?

5. What would you do if you had a friend who behaved like Benito did?

 Social Studies

Use a Map Look at a map of California. Locate Los Angeles in southern California and Redwood National Park in northern California. List some interesting places you might fly over if you flew from one of those places to the other.

School-Home Connection Tell a family member about this story. Then talk about some positive things that Benito could have done with his talent for basketball.

Word Count: 1,489